Cubs

Written by Sasha Morton

Collins

This fox cub has a log den.

den

This cub naps.

This cub gets a fish.

fish

This cub is hot.

rock

This cub has a long sip.

wet

/ng/

14

15

After reading

Letters and Sounds: Phase 3

Word count: 40

Focus phonemes: /w/ /x/ /sh/ /th/ /ng/

Common exception words: to, be, push

Curriculum links: Understanding the World: The World

Early learning goals: Understanding: answer "how" and "why" questions about their experiences and in response to stories or events; Reading: children use phonic knowledge to decode regular words and read them aloud accurately, read some common irregular words, demonstrate understanding when talking with others about what they have read

Developing fluency

- Your child may enjoy hearing you read the book.
- Look at page 12 together. Point to the exclamation mark. Explain that we can use exclamation marks to show surprise or excitement. This shows us that the text can be read in a particular way, with more expression and enthusiasm. Model reading the sentence. Now ask your child to read the sentence with expression.

Phonic practice

- Look at the inside front cover and point to the grapheme "th". Say the sound together.
- Now look at page 10 together. Ask your child if they can spot a word that contains "th". (*this*)
- Sound out the word together. Model using your finger to make a line under "th", a dot under "i" and a dot under "s" as you say the sounds.
- Look at the "I spy sounds" pages (14–15). Say the sounds together. How many items or descriptions can your child spot that contain the /ng/ sound? (*wing, young, morning*) Can they find any items with the /sh/ sound in them? (*fish, starfish, ship, shark, shrimp*)

Extending vocabulary

- Read each of the words below to your child. Can they find each word's opposite (antonym) in the list on the right?

push	wet
short	cold
dry	long
hot	pull